MW00975893

How I Survived Being Sex Trafficked
By Freda Young

Introduction

The names and places of this book have been changed to protect others, not the people who committed these evil acts, but others. Many things have been left out, considering other things I am not capable of processing at the moment, which would take many more years to deal with. If there are other things I do not have full complete memory of and that make me extremely uncomfortable, it will not be discussed.

I. Horror

Descent

I grew up in a home where there was nothing I wanted or needed that I did not already have. I was well taken care of. I started ballet at a young age, which trained me to match my ability to express myself through dance and music and coordinate both. To this day, I don't enjoy listening to only classical music, but if I danced to it as well, it becomes my favorite music. This was my passion, and I had excelled within ballet. At the age of 16, I was at the highest level of an international ballet company on the East Coast. My ballet teacher had spoken to me about finishing high school at their school. I, very foolishly, declined. With years and hours being solely dedicated to these activities, I never had time to spend time with friends, let alone have a social life. This influenced my decision to stay where I was and try to feel normal and "hang out" with friends. I look back on this decision with deep regret over and over many times to this day.

After I came home from the East Coast, I was at a party. My car was towed from parking in a spot that apparently was no parking. I needed a ride and a friend of the person who was hosting the party offered me a ride. I gladly said yes, but less than two minutes later while he was turning left, our car was hit in a head-on collision. I lost consciousness upon impact. I honestly don't know if I regained consciousness standing up, I don't remember getting out of the car. The ambulance came, me and the driver got into the ambulance, and then a week later I regained consciousness at a restaurant with my family. The doctors had said that from the accident, I now had multiple bulging discs and would never be able to dance ballet again. This is where a part of me died.

I have reason to believe this began a series of missing time and missing memories. I remember after that, someone from my high school said something extremely nasty about me. Since rumors were commonplace for these types of people, I just became very angry with them and started hanging out with other people. Those people were constantly high or drunk. That became my sole purpose. I was younger, but my best friend was 18, and so she would bring me around people in their 20s to party with. This normally consisted of me being encouraged to get blacked out drunk, and then her leaving me for some random man to have sex with me. I really thought nothing of it. Every time I was blamed because it was "my fault" that I was drunk, and their reasoning was I had the control to get that drunk, if I didn't want to have sex with someone, I wouldn't have become blackout drunk. With this wonderful thing of consistently getting blackout drunk each weekend, and random men having sex with me, some of these idiots had girlfriends. That made ME the slut, whore, etc, never would any of those women recognize or acknowledge that their precious boyfriend took advantage of a completely inebriated person.

With getting drunk on the weekends, I just wanted an escape to everyday life. This is when I met marijuana. I quickly realized (and this is back in early 2000s where there was no pot drive test) that I couldn't get a DUI. This solved all my problems I thought, because I could just stay high and not have to feel all of the pain that had been building up. Pot became what I lived for. It was the only thing that made me feel normal. Ironically, I believe that pot was going to make me okay, I never knew that my addiction would be the reason why I was placed in such dangerous situations.

I went on to complete one semester of college successfully. However, after another car accident, my second semester failed terribly. I felt that pot was the only thing to cope mentally after my head was shook up pretty good this second time as well. I was moved to another part of the country after I became black out drunk in front of my entire family during a family event and kept yelling things that were clearly impossible but very offensive. When I'm drunk, it's not "truth serum" like other people say, it's like I think I'm the president of Hawaii and other absurd things. While living in another part of the country, my family member I was living with literally had no money, and I had no money. I reached out to someone to beg for money so I could eat that day and got an absolute "no". I'll give them credit they probably believed I would only use it for drugs. This other friend said she was a stripper around my age when she was drunk, so I thought that was the only way for immediate cash considering Welfare has never helped me up to that point, so literally that actually is my only option. And also considering if I had gotten a job, it would still be more than two weeks, however long the first pay period is, for the first check to even be processed.

I went to a strip club for the first time, and found that it was addicting in another way. I began stripping anywhere that I was moved to. This was a very toxic environment, which I personally do not think is healthy. I believe it trains your subconscious to believe your worth (income) is based on sexually exploiting yourself. This was the "gateway drug" so to speak that led to me being sex trafficked.

Karen Vague

   I came back to the other part of the country. After a while, my body completely broke out in a skin disease (which is not contagious) but also distorts the skin and has growths on the top layer of my skin. This is why I was fired from the strip clubs there. This woman I met, Karen Vague, approached me and said I could live with her. At the time, I could not live at my home, because drugs were not allowed and I was heavy into my addiction, so I decided to stay with her. I'm not sure how long I was living with her in her parent's home until she said the only way I could work is if I sold myself for money. At the time, there was no money and for me to continue my dependency, this seemed like the only option for me to survive. The first pimp she set me up with was immediately arrested within five minutes of picking me up because he was in a stolen car. Karen decided to take me to another city around 5 hours away. When we arrived, the pimp got into the driver's seat and Karen sat in the passenger's seat. I do not know how long I was sex trafficked for, I don't even remember them taking pictures of me for the ads. I have one memory of Karen sitting in the hotel room sitting in a chair while this disgusting man had sex with me. She immediately took the money and said, "the pimp NEEDS it." I'm not sure how long this continued, but I do remember sitting at a gas station with Karen and the pimp and saying I don't want to do this anymore. They weren't giving me anything but throwing drugs at me, and I'm not even sure if I was even eating at the time. They kicked me out of the car and I blacked out and have no clue how I got home.

"Sure" the Pimp

A couple years later, I developed a new addiction, cocaine. Most of the people I was living with on their couches, did not allow this around. There was this man who came into the club I worked at, and only talked to me. I remember my friend trying to ask him for a dance and he basically told her to f*** off. He handed me a "consulting" card and told me to call him. I thought at that moment, because of the previous experience I could handle it. I didn't think twice about it. I had no clue that later he would demand money for my freedom.

I called the pimp and he picked me up. I had no ID at the time, and he told me to go into this hotel and check in. I said I have no ID and he said not to worry about it

and mentioned something I'm not allowed to say. Then
things got really blurry. I remember him taking pictures
of me and he had me buy a burner phone. He instructed
me that he would be placing ads of me and that I was to
answer the burner phone and give him all of the money.
This happened for I don't know how long. I would be
stuck in a hotel room, random sometimes very gross
men would have sex with me, and I gave him all the
money. Then, this one "john" I met came. He looked at
me very sadly and said he thought I should not be doing
this anymore. I thought he was crazy because I was
convinced this was going to continue until I finally died.
At that moment, I had a heavy depression where I
absolutely wanted to die, or figure out a way for someone
to kill me. He insisted. The john told me to get all my
belongings and leave with him. I left $1,000 from that
day in a part of the hotel, and left the burner phone. I
thought that would be more than enough for the pimp
because the previous pimp let me go. This pimp was
very angry. The pimp called me furious saying I owed
him money for my freedom. I slit my wrists and texted
him a picture saying I'd rather die than be sex trafficked
again. This didn't stop. I remember being in the
hospital screaming telling the doctors, police, and social
workers that a pimp was after me and they all ignored
me. I was still coming off of drugs and wasn't thinking
clearly, but I should have shown the authorities the texts

from the three different phone numbers telling me to "work" (be sex trafficked) again.

I remember taking bottles of my psychiatric medication and dumping 20 pills into my hand and taking them. I then woke up again, across the country, in a Detox center. I was then transferred to a rehab in another part of the country. Rehab began my recovery.

II. Coping

I fully believe rehab and therapy services are required for healing. I would not have been able to do it on my own. Dialectical Behavior Therapy skills are the main reason why I am able to cope with the world. The following is my own commentary how I implemented DBT into my life. Understand this is not what DBT explanations are, but my own opinion of how I personally use them. With the trauma of being sex trafficked it is very important to separate those events from your true self. Once you separate these moments you will be able to move on. Really focus on that this is something that happened to you, it is not who you are. Understand there is karma, which I will talk about in the next section, which no person is able to escape. When we take the time to remove the events from our focus, it enables us to move on and thrive. We will be stronger, not tortured, because those events will enable us to work through day to day situations with understanding that we are capable of healing and no one can stop that.

Here are some of the DBT skills:

MINDFULNESS (Wise Mind)

Using the What Skills:

-Observe
-Describe
-Participate

Observe what you are seeing. Pull yourself back into your body and really watch what is happening around you. Are there people around you? What does the room or environment look like? Be present and mindful.

Describe what you are seeing. How would you describe what you are sitting on? How would you describe what you are standing near? Describe how the air feels, what your emotions are. Truly feel the present moment.

Participate in what you are seeing. Can you start a conversation with someone around you? Can you write down your current emotions? Can you be active in what is going on around you? Participate in the present moment.

~

Using the How Skills:

-Non-judgmentally
-One-mindfully
-Effectively

Non-judgmentally: Approach things with an open mind. Try to expand your consciousness to be open to understanding things you may have wrongfully or in error judged. Bring about an open heart to become non-judgmental.

One-mindfully: Focus on pulling your consciousness fully together to be integrated as one. Breathe and think about controlling your mind to be combined and in the moment.

Effectively: Be effective in every action you take. Imagine success with a persistent approach. Be confident in all actions, thoughts, and words. Act like you are the most successful person you know and approach situations as if you are already that successful person you imagine yourself to be.

~

DISTRESS TOLERANCE

Using Crisis Survival: Distraction with Wise Mind Accepts

A: Activities
C: Contributing
C: Comparisons
E: Emotions Use Opposite
P: Pushing Away
T: Thoughts
S: Sensations

Activities: Think about what you enjoy. What makes you happy? Join a physical activity, a baseball team, basketball, dance, aerobics, yoga anything that gets you moving and out of your current head-space. Do you enjoy drawing, coloring, painting, or DYI projects? Put your focus into an activity that enables you to create a sense of accomplishment.

Contributing: Do something that blesses another person. Help a person by opening the door for them. Buy groceries for someone, help someone with something they've been struggling with. Volunteer at the local shelter, elderly retirement center, or any place that needs volunteers. Get out into the world and make a difference. This builds up wonderful karma.

Comparisons: Compare how much better your life has become versus the trauma of the past. You are now free and out of their reach. Understand there are positive experiences that have now shifted for you to be happy.

Emotions Use Opposite: If you are struggling with harsh emotions, which will happen with trauma, flip it like a switch in your brain to have the exact opposite. If you are angry, flip it to be compassionate. If you are sad, flip it to overwhelming joy. We do have the ability to control our emotions, there are situations where the trauma may be overwhelming and we have to wait until it passes, but if there is a chance to change it, take that change.

Pushing Away: Push away from your conscious the pain after accepting it. If the pain of the trauma comes, feel it and accept it. But if it comes again, just let it flow through you. Then you can push that emotion away because you already let it go and it now longer has a right to affect you.

Thoughts: Be mindful and understanding of every

thought that comes to you. I know from experience there are times where thoughts may seem completely uncontrollable. And that might happen, it might be too overwhelming and horrific to control. But with trial and error, we can eventually build up the strength to control our thoughts. But I do believe it takes time and practice. Change your thoughts to believe everything has a purpose and that you will get through the storm.

Sensations: With sensations there can be emotions evoked. Try to get yourself out of your current frame of mind with changing your physical situation. Get a pack of ice, hold it (not for too long only several minutes). Take a hot bath. Do some yoga stretches. Go for a run. Eat something you love. Change what you are emotionally feeling by adjusting your physical sensations.

~

Use **Self Soothe** with five senses:

-**Taste**
-**Smell**
-**See**
-**Hear**
-**Touch**

Taste: Eat something you love. Cook your favorite meal. Go to your favorite restaurant.

Smell: Use essential oils. Smell your favorite perfume. Buy some flowers.

See: Put yourself in an environment where there is something you desire to see. Watch your favorite TV show or movie. Go to the mall and look at clothing or items you admire.

Hear: Listen to your favorite music. Go see a live band. Listen to a book on tape. Find a self-help video online.

Touch: Create something with clay. Create a college of a wish board of things you desire in your life. Attend to a garden. Clean and do chores to change your environment for the better.

Using **Improve the Moment**:

-I: Imagery
-M: Meaning
-P: Prayer
-R: Relaxation

-**O:** One Thing at a Time
-**V**: Vacation
-**E:** Encouragement

Imagery: Imagine yourself as the most powerful man or woman that you want to be. See yourself as a beautiful creation that is here for a purpose to help. Imagine everything you want in your life. Every thought that can be created for the better can affect our reality in the future. Create as many thoughts by imaging the best of the best circumstances for your life.

Meaning: Find the meaning in all things. I don't fully believe everything happens for a reason, but I do believe that everything that happens can be flipped to be a blessing, no matter how evil or traumatic the past has been.

Prayer: Pray to who you find to be your Higher Power. This can take many forms, whether it is the Most High God, Father God, a goddess, Gaia, the Universe, anyone you are drawn to. That is your personal journey. Pray to that Higher Power that things improve. You can pray that it benefits you instead of continuing to harm you in anyway. You can pray the Higher Power takes over and deals with the situation. Prayer is the best way to let go of things we cannot control.

Relaxation: Find a situation where you are truly relaxed. Think about what environment you need to be in to relax. Surround yourself with people who relax you. Sink into that moment of being calm and collected.

One Thing at a Time: Focus on one thing at a time, literally. Don't move onto the next item, thought, or action until you dealt with the first thing that has come up. Write a list on each item or concern in order that it appears. Deal with each item in order of where it appears, from top to bottom.

Vacation: Take a vacation. Go somewhere to get your mind off things. Visit a forest, go to the beach, visit the lake. If finances are an issue, visit some body of water to heal. For me, surrounding myself with some form of water and meditating while I'm there helps. I focus on mentally placing all my problems into the water, for the problems to dissolve.

Encouragement: Encourage yourself. Surround yourself with encouraging people letting you know that you can and will succeed despite the trauma. If there are no encouraging people, focus on encouraging yourself. Know that you are better than what has happened. Know that you are stronger than what has happened.

Know that you will succeed regardless of all circumstances.

~

Using Pros and Cons

Try to find the Pros and then Cons of a situation you are facing. Write them on a blackboard, write them on your mirror with a dry erase marker, write them on a piece of paper, whatever is the most visually powerful for you. Go through the situation to find if it is beneficial or detrimental before you make your choice.

~

Using Accepting Reality

Accept reality regardless of how painful it is. There are moments personally for me where I cannot stay in reality and go into my own version of reality. It takes time for when I can come back, but I just essentially wasted a bunch of time not accepting the past. So if you can avoid this, and focus on just accepting the reality of the past by separating yourself from it, you will heal. Personally, I force myself into a thought process of, "Is that the best you can do?" to my abusers. I survived. You survived. We will claim victory over everyday life. Focus on being the best you can be. Frank Sinatra even said, "The best revenge is massive success."

~

Willingness

Have willingness to make a change for the better in all possible ways in your life. Be willing to conquer your fear and trauma with prayer, acceptance, and bravery. Know that you have the ability to be willing to be successful. Everything we think, we can do. Be willing to change your mindset. Be willing to accept help. Be willing to heal.

~

Turning Your Mind

Turn your mind by shifting your thought patterns. Try to meditate to do a 180 if you are struggling. Focus on turning your mind to success, love, and happiness.

~

Radical Acceptance

Radically accept all past events and current situations. There is nothing you can't think your way out of. Try to motivate yourself to activate an intelligence you might have suppressed. With radically accepting hard things, you are able to hold it and shift it to what you want out of future circumstances. You have the power and strength to radically accept all situations.

~

EMOTIONAL REGULATION

Using Reduce Vulnerability

Reduce vulnerability by empowering yourself. Strengthen yourself by focusing on calling yourself to a higher calling. You can help others with the situations you have been in. Know you are called to be a survivor, no longer a victim. We might have definitely been victimized in past events, but we don't have to stay a victim. Focus on the power that is available to everyone who has been victimized. I believe our universe has a law of balance. If things became unbalanced, by horrible circumstances, greatness can now be called because it is what every survivor is called to.

~

P & L: Treat Physical Illness
-E: Eating
-A: Altering Drugs (no drugs unless it is medication to be taken as prescribed by your doctor)
-S: Sleep
-E: Exercise

P & L: Treat Physical Illness: Go to the doctor. Exercise. Treat your body with care. Be attentive to any issues or concerns you have. Take care of your body, it's one you have to live in.

E: Eating: Focus on the foods you eat. If you want to choose to be vegetarian or vegan, follow your truth. If you choose to eat any other way, enjoy every meal.

A: Altering Drugs: Avoid all mood altering drugs unless prescribed by a doctor. I personally do not smoke marijuana anymore, firstly because it was a major cause for terrible circumstances for me, but also it is a mild psychedelic. I do not tend to have any psychedelics in my system, because I do personally believe it opens you to the astral realm in an unnatural way. There are other psychedelics that are used medically, but that is under the supervision of a doctor or shaman which I understand. I personally don't go there.

-S: Sleep: Take care of your body by sleeping with sleep cycles that improve your life. Sleep is a way for our brain to recharge. This helps us mentally throughout the day and heal.

-E: Exercise: Get your body moving in any way possible. Yoga, baseball, basketball, dance, aerobics, running, anything that gets your blood pumping.

~

Using Build Mastery

Do something that creates a sense of accomplishment. Take a free online course with Coursera. Find a subject you want to explore. Paint, create a piece of art, sculpt something. Find an accreditation you want. All of these activities can greatly improve your sense of worth and self.

~

Build Positive Experiences

Interact with the world that improves your view on the

world to be safe and nurturing. Meet new friends that are safe and helpful, people you enjoy being around who lift you up.

~

Be Mindful of Current Emotion

What are you currently feeling? What do you want to be feeling? If you need to take a moment to process your current emotion, do so safely. Focus on the emotions of success and happiness.

~

Opposite to Emotion Action

Do an action that is the exact opposite of your emotion if the emotion is negative or upsetting. If you feel like sleeping all day, push yourself to get up, take a shower or bath, and get ready for the day. Distract yourself with reading, watching a favorite TV show, creating an art or craft.

~

INTERPERSONAL EFFECTIVENESS

Using Objectiveness Effectiveness

DEAR MAN
-**D:** Describe
-**E:** Express
-**A**: Assert
-**R:** Reinforce
-**M:** Mindful
-**A**: Appear Confident
-**N:** Negotiate

-**D:** Describe: Describe the situation you are currently in.
-**E:** Express: Express your emotions with this current situation.
-**A:** Assert: Assert your current feelings or emotions about the situation.
-**R:** Reinforce: Make it known about your concerns or thoughts about the situation.
-**M:** Mindful: Be mindful about how you are coming across in appearance or demeanor to others.
-**A:** Appear Confident: Draw strength to yourself and appear confident. Focus on the goal of the situation of what you want.
-**N:** Negotiate: Negotiate what you want to have. Say your thoughts and feelings and argue your case for

yourself. Be your own advocate.

~

Using Relationship Effectiveness (GIVE)

-G: Gentle
-I: Interested
-V: Validate
-E: Easy Manner

-G: Gentle: Be gentle in the situation. Use calmness when speaking and thinking.
-I: Interested: Show your interest in what is happening. Show what you desire through your interest.
-V: Validate: Validate your own emotions and feelings. You don't have to wait for others to validate you. Be strong and know this validation you deserve you give to yourself.
-E: Easy Manner: Have an easy manner when discussing the situation. Be calm, cool, and collected.

~

Self-Respect Effectiveness (FAST)

-F: Fair
-A: Apologies (No Apologies)

-S: Stick to Value
-T: Truthful

-F: Fair: Be fair in the situation. Look at both sides of the situation.

-A: Apologies (No Apologies): Make the situation so there is no necessary reason to apologize for anything unnecessary or that is not your fault. I personally believe if there is a situation that does require your apology, then an apology should happen. But do not put yourself in that situation if you can control it.

-S: Stick to Value: Hold fast to what you believe are your values and important to you.

-T: Truthful: Be truthful in all things. I do believe in something called the Akashic record, where all of our actions are recorded in another dimension, that no human can change. Be fearless in holding fast to the truth in all things.

III. Spiritual Aspects

I believe there are beings higher than us that do observe us and they do have the capability of intervening on our behalf, especially if we are placed in dangerous situations. The Bible states in Hebrew 12:1-2 "Therefore, since we are surrounded by such a great cloud of witnesses, let us throw off everything that hinders and the sin that so easily entangles. And let us run with perseverance the race marked out for us, fixing our eyes on Jesus, the pioneer and perfecter of faith." Whatever your Higher Power is, gain a relationship with that Higher Power.

I do also believe in karma. I think this is an important life aspect that all people need to consider. Whatever you call it yourself, it is the concept that each action has a reaction of equal or greater force. Keep in your heart that whatever has happened to you, will be brought to justice, whether in this life directly, or it will have a greater impact in the next life. People who do horrific things will have consequences. Call upon your Higher Power for justice and to bring action to the situation.

Personally for me, I have found comfort in Jesus, whom I call Yehusha. I call my Higher Power the Most High God and Yahuah. I refer to the Holy Spirit as the Ruach. I plead the blood of Yehusha over my life, to redeem me from everything I have been through. Yehusha is my comforter and the upholder of my life. In the book of Psalms it says, "He rescued me from my strong enemy, and from those who hated me, for they were too mighty for me. They confronted me in the day of my calamity, but the LORD was my support. He brought me out into a broad place; he rescued me; because he delighted in me." Yehusha is truly mighty to save, and my life has truly been proof of this.

Anyone can pray prayers of protection and call upon Yahuah. In Psalm 91 it states, "He who dwells in the shelter of the Most High will abide in the shadow of the Almighty. I will say to the LORD, "My refuge and my fortress, my God is whom I trust." For He will deliver you from the snare of the fowler and from the deadly pestilence. He will cover you with His pinions, and under His wings you will find refuge; His faithfulness is a shield and buckler. You will not fear the terror of the night, nor the arrow that flies by day, nor the pestilence that stalks in the darkness, nor the destruction that wastes at noonday. A thousand may fall at your side, ten thousand at your right hand, but it will not come near you. You will only look with your eyes and see the recompense of the wicked. Because you have made the LORD your dwelling place- the Most High, who is my refuge- no evil shall be allowed to befall you, no plague come near your tent. For He will command His angels concerning you to guard you in all your ways. On their hands they will bear you up, lest you strike your foot against a stone. You will tread on the lion and the adder; the young lion and the serpent you will trample underfoot. "Because he holds fast to Me in love, I will deliver him; I will protect him, because he knows My name. When he calls to me, I will answer him; I will be with him in trouble; I will rescue him and honor him. With long life I will satisfy him, and show him My salvation." Praying this Psalm has greatly helped me cope with all of the pain and fear.

The last Psalm I want to share that has been proven to work in my life is Psalm 35:1-3 "Contend, O LORD, with those who contend with me; fight against those who fight against me! Take hold of shield and buckler and rise for my help! Draw the spear and javelin against my pursuers! Say to my soul, I am your salvation!" Yehusha is my guide, he is my strength, and He has saved me. I pray for all sex trafficking victims that Yahuah is your strength and guides you to heal fully and lead a successful, amazing life.

I want to close this book with a prayer for all sex trafficked victims:

"I cry out to the Most High God, in the name of Yehusha Hamashiach, that you would forgive all of our sins, known and unknown by the blood of Yehusha Hamaschiach. I pray that you heal all of our wounds, for you say in Isaiah 53:5, "But he was bruised for our inquities: the chastisement of our peace was upon him; and with his stripes we are healed." In the name of Yeshua Hamashiach I pray boldness, strength, and determination in having our experiences been turned into a blessing for those who are still suffering. Most High God I pray you complete your promise for us that you said in Joel 2:25, " So I will restore to you the years that the locust has eaten,...". Please bless us with that which was taken from us by tragic experiences. I pray Yahuah that you would guide us, bless us, and take us under the shadow of your wings. In Yehusha Hamashiach's name."

Made in the USA
Columbia, SC
16 May 2020

97444566R00021